FINDING A VOICE:
Women's Fight for Equality in U.S. Society

THE FEMINIST MOVEMENT TODAY

ELIZABETH KING HUMPHREY

FINDING A VOICE:
Women's Fight for Equality in U.S. Society

TITLES IN THIS SERIES

THE FEMINIST
MOVEMENT TODAY

ELIZABETH KING HUMPHREY

MASON CREST
PHILADELPHIA

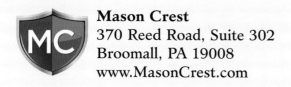

Mason Crest
370 Reed Road, Suite 302
Broomall, PA 19008
www.MasonCrest.com

Printed and bound in the United States of America.

CPSIA Compliance Information: Batch #FF2012-9. For further information, contact Mason Crest at 1-866-MCP-Book.

First printing
1 3 5 7 9 8 6 4 2

Library of Congress Cataloging-in-Publication Data

Humphrey, Elizabeth King.
  The feminist movement today / Elizabeth King Humphrey.
     p. cm. — (Finding a voice: women's fight for equality in U.S. society)
  Includes bibliographical references and index.
  ISBN 978-1-4222-2352-9 (hc)
  ISBN 978-1-4222-2362-8 (pb)
  1. Feminism—United States—History—21st century—Juvenile literature. I. Title.
  HQ1421.H86 2012
  305.42097309'05—dc23
                              2011043482

Picture credits: Office of Senator Barbara Boxer: 47 (left); Collection of the Supreme Court of the United States: 39, 41; office of Senator Susan Collins: 47 (right); © iStockphoto.com / Kate Husa: 19; Library of Congress: 16, 18, 20, 21; office of Senator Patty Murray: 47 (center); National Aeronautics and Space Administration: 26, 28, 29, 30; courtesy Ronald Reagan Presidential Library: 37; Arindambanerjee / Shutterstock.com: 23; Ryan Rodrick Beiler / Shutterstock.com: 45; Steve Broer / Shutterstock.com: 48; Cheryl Casey / Shutterstock.com: 54; Creatista / Shutterstock.com: 3; Jose Gil / Shutterstock.com: 51, 53; K2 images / Shutterstock.com: 40; Lev Radin / Shutterstock.com: 13; used under license from Shutterstock.com: 8; U.S. Air Force photo: 31, 32 (center); U.S. Army photo: 32 (left); courtesy U.S. Department of State: 52; U.S. Marine Corps photo: 32 (right); U.S. Navy photo: 34, 57; courtesy Women's Rights National Historical Park, National Park Service: 17.

TABLE OF CONTENTS

INTRODUCTION

As the Executive Director of the Sewall-Belmont House & Museum, which is the fifth and final headquarters of the historic National Woman's Party (NWP), I am surrounded each day by artifacts that give voice to the stories of Alice Paul, Lucy Burns, Doris Stevens, Alva Belmont, and the whole community of women who waged an intense campaign for the right to vote during the second decade of the 20th century. The

A. Page Harrington, director, Sewall-Belmont House & Museum

original photographs, documents, protest banners, and magnificent floor-length capes worn by these courageous activists during marches and demonstrations help us bring their work to life for the many groups who tour the museum each week.

The perseverance of the suffragists bore fruit in 1920, with the ratification of the 19th Amendment. It was a huge milestone, though certainly not the end of the journey toward full equality for American women.

Throughout much (if not most) of American history, social conventions and the law constrained female participation in the political, economic, and intellectual life of the nation. Women's voices were routinely stifled, their contributions downplayed or dismissed, their potential ignored. Underpinning this state of affairs was a widely held assumption of male superiority in most spheres of human endeavor.

Always, however, there were women who gave the lie to gender-based stereotypes. Some helped set the national agenda. For example, in the years preceding the Revolutionary War, Mercy Otis Warren made a compelling case for American independence through her writings. Abigail Adams, every bit the intellectual equal of her husband, counseled John Adams to "remember the ladies and be more generous and favorable to them than your ancestors" when creating laws for the new country. Sojourner Truth helped lead the movement to abolish slavery in the 19th century. A hundred years later, Rosa Parks galvanized the civil rights movement, which finally secured for African Americans the promise of equality under the law.

The lives of these women are familiar today. So, too, are the stories of groundbreakers such as astronaut Sally Ride; Supreme Court justice Sandra Day O'Connor; and Nancy Pelosi, Speaker of the House of Representatives.

But famous figures are only part of the story. The path toward gender equality was also paved—and American society shaped—by countless women whose individual lives and deeds have never been chronicled in depth. These include the women who toiled alongside their fathers and brothers and husbands on the western frontier; the women who kept U.S. factories running during World War II; and the women who worked tirelessly to promote the goals of the modern feminist movement.

The FINDING A VOICE series tells the stories of famous and anonymous women alike. Together these volumes provide a wide-ranging overview of American women's long quest to achieve full equality with men—a quest that continues today.

The Sewall-Belmont House & Museum is located at 144 Constitution Avenue in Washington, D.C. You can find out more on the Web at www.sewallbelmont.org

According to the U.S. Department of Labor, in 2011 women made up about 47 percent of the labor force. However, despite laws outlawing discrimination on the basis of gender, it has been difficult for women to break through the "glass ceiling" and achieve promotion to the most powerful, prestigious, and highest-paying positions.

1

QUESTIONS OF FAIRNESS

I magine this: You apply for a job. You are perfectly qualified. But the company refuses even to consider you. The reason? You are a woman with preschool-age kids. Regardless of any child-care arrangements you've made, the company assumes you won't be a reliable employee. And anyway, your place is in the home. Your proper role is to look after your children. No such assumptions are made about men with young children, though. The company doesn't hesitate to hire fathers with preschool-age children.

Or imagine this: You are a married woman, and you and your husband own a house together. After your husband gets into some trouble with the law, you separate. Your husband hires a lawyer to represent him in his criminal case. But the lawyer wants a guarantee that he'll be paid. Without telling you, your husband puts your home up as security. This means that, should your husband fail to pay his legal bills, the lawyer would get ownership of part of your home. You find out about this arrangement only after you and your husband divorce. And as it turns out, your ex-husband hasn't paid his legal bills. His lawyer now demands that you pay. When you refuse, the lawyer asks the local sheriff to take possession of your house and sell it. To your shock, you discover that the law is on his side. In your state, a married man is considered the "head and master" of the household. As such, he legally controls all property owned jointly with his wife. He is free to do whatever he wishes with his and his wife's house, cars, bank account, and more. Under the law, a wife gets no say. So when your former husband put up your house as security for his legal debt, he was perfectly within his rights.

It's not hard to see why these two situations would be unfair. In each instance, women would be placed at a disadvantage relative to men. For no reason other than gender, women would have less freedom than men to make decisions affecting their lives.

Recent opinion polls show that, by a very large majority, Americans favor gender equality. In other words, they believe that men and women should have equal rights and opportunities. And the United States has laws against discrimination (unequal treatment) based on gender. But this hasn't always been true. In fact, the two examples of unfair treatment outlined above aren't made up. They are actual cases. And they happened not so long ago.

YOUNG MOTHERS NEED NOT APPLY

In 1966, a married woman named Ida Phillips answered a help-wanted ad in a Florida newspaper. It was for a trainee position at a large company called Martin Marietta Corporation. Phillips was told that her application wouldn't be accepted because she had a child under six years of age.

Two years earlier, the U.S. Congress had passed, and President Lyndon B. Johnson had signed, the Civil Rights Act of 1964. This law made it illegal for employers to discriminate against individuals based on their "race, color, religion, sex, or national origin." Ida Phillips thought Martin Marietta's refusal to consider her for a job was discrimination based on her sex. She sued the company.

A district court in Florida threw out the lawsuit. The court pointed out that about three-quarters of the people hired for the position Phillips sought were women. What that meant, in the court's view, was that Martin Marietta didn't discriminate against women. Phillips appealed. But the appeals court refused to reconsider the decision.

THE EQUAL RIGHTS AMENDMENT

The 1960s and 1970s saw major gains in equality for American women. Congress passed laws aimed at promoting fairness in the workplace. A series of court rulings chipped away at different forms of discrimination against women. Long-held beliefs that women were not suited for leadership roles began to change.

But many women's-rights advocates grew frustrated with the slow pace of progress. They wanted a measure that, once and for all, would demonstrate the nation's unshakable commitment to gender equality. They focused on changing the U.S. Constitution through an amendment. They campaigned for adoption of the Equal Rights Amendment (ERA).

The idea of enshrining gender equality in the Constitution wasn't new. A women's-rights leader named Alice Paul first proposed a version of the ERA in 1923. But it's not easy to change the Constitution. A proposed amendment must first win a two-thirds majority in both the U.S. Senate and House of Representatives. Then it is sent to the states for ratification, or approval. Three-quarters (38 of 50) states must ratify the amendment, usually within seven years, for it to take effect.

It wasn't until 1972 that the ERA passed in the Senate and House of Representatives. The proposed amendment read:

Section 1. Equality of rights under the law shall not be denied or abridged by the United States or by any state on account of sex.

Section 2. The Congress shall have the power to enforce, by appropriate legislation, the provisions of this article.

Section 3. This amendment shall take effect two years after the date of ratification.

At first, the ERA appeared well on its way to approval. Thirty of the required 38 states had ratified the amendment by the end of 1973. But as opponents organized, support stalled. With the March 1979 deadline for ratification looming, the amendment was still three states short. Congress extended the deadline to June 1982, to no avail. The ERA fell three state ratifications short.

The case ended up before the Supreme Court. In January 1971, the Court issued its decision in the case of *Phillips v. Martin Marietta Corp*. In the decision, the Court made note of the fact that Martin Marietta hired men with preschool-age children. This didn't necessarily violate the Civil Rights Act. Under the law, a company could treat males and females differently. But the company would have to show that this was "reasonably necessary to the normal operation" of its business. (A menswear company, for example, wouldn't be expected to hire women to model its clothing.) Did Martin Marietta's hiring practices meet the legal standard? In the Supreme Court's view, no. Company officials might reasonably believe that having small children could cause employees' job performance to suffer. Such employees, for example, might miss more days of work caring for sick kids. If this was a concern, Martin Marietta could have a policy against hiring parents with young kids. But the company couldn't just refuse to hire women with young kids. It couldn't assume that child care was a woman's duty.

The Supreme Court ruled that hiring policies such as Martin Marietta's were against the law. In so doing, the Court struck a blow for equality in the workplace.

A CASE OF EQUAL PROTECTION

In the case known as *Kirchberg v. Feenstra*, the issue wasn't workplace equality. Rather, it was fairness with regard to the property rights of married couples.

FAST FACT

In 1960, a 28-year-old secretary named Lois Rabinowitz went to a New York City traffic court to pay a $10 ticket for her boss. But the judge threw Rabinowitz out of the courtroom. The reason? She was wearing slacks, which the judge considered unladylike.

In 1966, Harold and Joan Feenstra bought a home together in Orleans Parish, Louisiana. About eight years later, their marriage fell apart. Harold Feenstra was arrested. He hired a lawyer, Karl J. Kirchberg, to represent him. Feenstra took out a second mortgage (loan) on the home he and his wife owned. The second mortgage served as security that Feenstra would pay Kirchberg. Feenstra didn't inform his wife about any of this. But under Louisiana law, he didn't have to. There—and in several other states—married women had no legal rights when it came to property they owned jointly with their husbands. Harold Feenstra could do whatever he wished with the home he and his wife owned.

Eventually, the criminal charges against Harold Feenstra were dropped. The Feenstras divorced.

Harold Feenstra moved out of Louisiana, leaving $3,000 in unpaid legal bills. In 1976, Karl Kirchberg contacted Joan Feenstra. He demanded that she pay the money her ex-husband owed. Kirchberg informed her of the second mortgage on her home, which he now held. If she didn't pay, Kirchberg threatened to foreclose on the mortgage and sell the house.

Rep. Carolyn Maloney of New York has re-introduced the Equal Rights Amendment at every session of the House of Representatives since 1997. However, the House has not voted on the proposed legislation since 1983. During her years in Congress, Maloney has been very active on issues involving women, children, and families.

When Joan Feenstra refused to pay the $3,000, Kirchberg followed through on his threat. He got a court order directing the local sheriff to seize and sell Feenstra's home.

In response, Feenstra challenged the Louisiana state law by which a husband was automatically deemed "head and master" of the household, with complete authority over a married couple's jointly owned property. The case eventually ended up before the Supreme Court. In 1981, the Court ruled in favor of Joan Feenstra. The Court struck down all state laws that deprived married women of the right to make decisions regarding joint property. Such laws, the Court said, violated the Equal Protection Clause of the U.S. Constitution.

A LONG STRUGGLE

For women in the United States, the struggle for equality has been long and difficult. That struggle has been fought on several fronts. Many important battles have occurred in the courts—the Phillips and Kirchberg cases are just two examples. The struggle has been waged in the halls of Congress. There, women have fought to get guarantees of gender equality written into the nation's laws. In the workplace, women have pushed for the opportunity to decide their own career paths. They've demanded to be allowed to go as far as their individual talents and ambition can take them. Many long-standing professional barriers have been broken. No less important, the struggle for gender equality has involved changing traditional social attitudes. These attitudes relegated women—and men—to roles "appropriate" to their gender.

Though many people believe that the work of gender equality is not yet completed, there is no denying that great progress has been made. Much of the credit goes to the feminist movement.

2

A BRIEF HISTORY OF THE FEMINIST MOVEMENT

The term *feminism* has several definitions. Organized activity in support of women's rights is one. Another is belief in the political, social, and economic equality of the sexes. Nothing in either definition excludes males. Men can work to ensure the rights of women. Men can believe that all people should be treated equally. So men can be feminists.

People who study the struggle for women's rights in the United States often divide the feminist movement into three major periods, or waves. This approach has limitations, and it's important to keep them in mind.

First, saying when each wave began or ended is difficult. Experts disagree on the dates. Some don't even believe it's helpful to think about the feminist movement in terms of waves. Instead, they see the struggle for gender equality as a continuous process.

Second, while each wave is said to have a major objective or focus, that is a bit of an oversimplification. Historical movements rarely fit into neat categories. The feminist movement is no exception. Feminists have never been completely unified in their concerns, goals, or strategies.

Still, considering the three waves of feminism is a useful exercise. It can provide context for the women's movement in the United States.

THE FIRST WAVE: VOTING RIGHTS

The first wave of the American feminist movement is generally said to have begun in the mid-1800s. The struggle for women's equality was inspired, at least in part, by another burning issue of the time: slavery.

Lucretia Mott

In 1840, the World Anti-Slavery Convention was held in London, England. It brought together abolitionists (people who wanted to get rid of slavery) from across the globe. The largest non-British delegation came from the United States. Among the American group were a half-dozen women. They included Lucretia Mott, a well-known American abolitionist. For years, Mott had been speaking, writing, and organizing to end slavery in the United States. Despite this, the World Anti-Slavery Convention refused to seat her—or any of the other women who had traveled to London for the meeting. Convention organizers didn't think women were fit to discuss the weighty subject of slavery.

Mott was outraged. So too was Elizabeth Cady Stanton. The 25-year-old was on her honeymoon. Her husband, Henry Stanton, was a delegate to the World Anti-Slavery Convention. In London, Elizabeth Cady Stanton met Lucretia Mott. The two struck up a friendship. They resolved to hold a convention to address the question of women's rights.

Elizabeth Cady Stanton

That convention was finally held eight years later, in Seneca Falls, New York. About 300 people, including 40 men, attended. The Seneca Falls Convention approved 11 resolutions, or statements. One of them proclaimed it the duty of American women to obtain for themselves the right to vote. At the time, the idea that the right to vote should extend to women was considered radical.

Susan B. Anthony

This monument at Women's Rights National Historical Park in Seneca Falls, New York, reproduces the "Declaration of Sentiments," along with the names of those who signed it.

The Seneca Falls Convention also produced a "Declaration of Sentiments." Written by Elizabeth Cady Stanton, it was modeled after the Declaration of Independence. It listed a broad range of ways men had established "absolute tyranny" over women. These included depriving women of property rights, job choices, and educational opportunities. The Declaration of Sentiments also condemned the denial of voting rights to women.

In the decades after the Seneca Falls Convention, women's-rights activists would direct much of their efforts toward gaining voting rights. That's why the first wave of the feminist movement is commonly thought of as the women's suffrage movement. (Suffrage is the right to vote.)

Women set up organizations to secure the right to vote. In 1869, Elizabeth Cady Stanton and Susan B. Anthony formed the National

Woman Suffrage Association. It favored an amendment to the U.S. Constitution that would guarantee all women in the country the right to vote. Meanwhile, Lucy Stone headed the American Woman Suffrage Association. If favored securing voting rights on a state-by-state basis.

Some gains were, in fact, made at the state or territorial level. In 1869, the Wyoming Territory granted women full voting rights. Utah, Colorado, and Idaho soon followed. Nationally, however, there was still much opposition to women suffrage.

In 1911, women won the right to vote in California. Arizona and Oregon granted women suffrage the following year.

Around the same time, suffragists—as women advocating for voting rights were called—stepped up their efforts nationwide. In 1913, an organization that would become known as the National Woman's Party was founded by Alice Paul and Lucy Burns. Its members organized large demonstrations and marches. They pressured lawmakers. They engaged in acts of civil disobedience.

These and other efforts bore fruit in 1919. On June 4 of that year, Congress passed the 19th Amendment to the Constitution. It guaranteed American women equal voting rights with men. The amendment was rati-

Alice Paul raises a glass to celebrate ratification of the Nineteenth Amendment to the U.S. Constitution, which gave women the right to vote. Paul's National Woman's Party was instrumental in getting the amendment passed into law in 1920.

fied on August 18, 1920. Many people say that milestone marked the end of the first wave of the feminist movement.

THE SECOND WAVE: WOMEN'S LIBERATION

The beginning of the feminist movement's second wave is generally dated to the 1960s. At the time, the civil rights movement was under way. African Americans, especially in the South, had long been treated as second-class citizens. The civil rights movement aimed to change that.

Many women saw that they, too, were treated as second-class citizens. Across American society, their voices were largely ignored. Few women held elective office. There were just 20 female members of Congress in 1960, for example.

Women faced a lot of discrimination in the business world. Companies kept them out of leadership and management positions. Higher-paying jobs were routinely reserved for men. When men and women did the same work, women's wages were lower.

There were strong social expectations about the way a woman should live her life. They centered on marriage and motherhood. It was widely assumed that a woman could find true fulfillment only by supporting her husband and raising her children, even if she also had to work outside the home to bring in some money. Middle-class women were expected to be full-time homemakers. A woman who didn't marry was likely to be regarded as an object of curiosity or pity. A woman who pursued a high-profile professional career would often be labeled strange or unfeminine.

During the 1950s and 1960s, most American women were expected to stay at home as mothers and housewives, rather than engaging in work outside the home.

Author and activist Betty Friedan (1921–2006) helped to start the "second wave" of American feminism during the 1960s.

In 1963, a book titled *The Feminine Mystique* was published. In it, author Betty Friedan challenged some widely held assumptions. Friedan interviewed house-wives for her book. Many admitted they were unhappy with their lives. She conclud-ed, "We can no longer ignore that voice within women that says: 'I want something more than my husband and my children and my home.'" According to Friedan, women needed challenging careers and educational opportunities in order to find fulfillment.

The Feminine Mystique helped fuel America's second wave of feminism. Today, the second wave is often referred to as the women's liberation movement. But this is misleading. The second wave had several currents. The women's liberation movement was simply the most famous. Its members demanded to be liberated, or freed, from the yoke of male domination.

All second-wave feminists wanted to get rid of the barriers standing in the way of career success for women. Feminists insisted that women receive the same educational opportunities as men. They said a woman should be free to pursue any career she chose. They demanded that women receive equal treatment in the workplace. This meant having the same chances as men to be hired and promoted. It also meant getting paid as much as men for the same work.

Feminists wanted to see changes in the home as well. They said that men should share in housework and child-care duties.

In 1966, Betty Friedan and 27 other feminists founded the National Organization for Women (NOW). Its mission statement declared: "The purpose of NOW is to take action to bring women into full participation in the mainstream of American society now, exercising all privileges and responsibilities thereof in truly equal partnership with men." NOW would become the largest women's-rights organization in the United States. It mobilized members to create political pressure for laws that guaranteed women's rights. It helped bring court challenges to unfair practices. NOW's leaders thought that working within the existing political system was the best way to win equality for women.

Many in the women's liberation movement disagreed. They thought that all of society's institutions were set up to serve the male power structure. So working for reform within the system wouldn't end the oppression of women. Rather, the entire social order had to be upended.

By the mid-1970s, the feminist movement was deeply divided. Mainstream feminists wanted to concentrate on goals such as equality in education and employment. Radical feminists, meanwhile, attacked traditional gender roles. They criticized marriage and motherhood. They railed against notions of female beauty. In the view of mainstream feminists, these kinds of positions were a distraction. They could cause a backlash

With banners demanding equality, women march through Washington, D.C., 1970.

FAST FACT

Twenty-eight women founded the National Organization for Women in 1966. By 2011, NOW's membership stood at more than half a million.

against the entire feminist movement. They hurt the chances for progress. Radical feminists countered that the mainstream of the movement wasn't doing enough to change the male power structure.

Mainstream feminist groups such as NOW made a big push for the Equal Rights Amendment. But political conservatives effectively mobilized to defeat the ERA. They claimed that the amendment was an attack on the family. In 1982, the ERA went down to defeat. It was a crushing blow for the feminist movement. And many people say it marked the end of the second wave.

FEMINISM TODAY: THE THIRD WAVE

The third wave of the feminist movement is generally said to have begun in the early 1990s. It continues to the present.

What is the third wave about? That's not an easy question to answer. Third-wave feminism embraces more diversity than did the previous waves. Many women who identify with the third wave say they are seeking individual empowerment. They are less concerned with being part of a unified movement.

Still, some general statements about the third wave can be made. The third wave has been driven largely by women who were born during or after the second wave. These younger women benefited from the gains secured by second-wave feminists. They grew up enjoying a higher degree of equality with males. They had more educational and professional opportunities than did their mothers. Many second-generation feminists complain that third-wavers take these gains for granted.

For their part, many third-wave feminists have been highly critical of the second wave. One common complaint is that the second wave was too focused on the concerns of white, middle-class women. The second wave, critics say, largely ignored the concerns of women of color and poor women. It also centered on women in the United States. Another complaint—whether valid or not—is that second-wave feminists tended to put down women who chose the traditional role of homemaker. It was assumed that women should pursue a professional career.

Third-wave feminists avoid saying there is just one understanding of what it means to be a woman. They think each woman should be able to create a kind of feminism relevant to her own situation. Third-wave feminists recognize the importance of race, ethnicity, and class to a woman's identity. Many have emphasized how these factors can magnify the effects of sexism, or discrimination based on gender. It is likely, for example, that a poor African-American or Latina woman will face more barriers to success than a middle-class white woman.

Many women who identify with the third wave say that feminism should be about justice for everyone. They believe feminists should be at the fore-

Today, many women actively protest against social injustices. However, their activities are more likely to be directed toward improving society for everyone, rather than being focused solely on gender issues. These young women are participating in an "Occupy Wall Street" protest against economic injustices, October 2011.

LILLY LEDBETTER'S STORY

Title VII of the Civil Rights Act of 1964 made it illegal for businesses to discriminate against women or minorities in employment. But the passage of that landmark law didn't wipe out such discrimination. Some businesses managed to hide their unfair practices.

That was a lesson Lilly Ledbetter learned. Ledbetter, who was born in 1938, went to work at the Goodyear Tire and Rubber plant in Gadsden, Alabama, in 1979. She was an overnight supervisor at the plant for almost 20 years.

Ledbetter got good job reviews. In 1996, she was honored with Goodyear's Top Performance Award. Two years later, as she was about to retire, someone at the Goodyear plant passed Ledbetter an unsigned note. It said that she was making less money than men who did the same job. Ledbetter investigated. She found out that the note was true. She'd been receiving less than her male colleagues for a long time.

Ledbetter filed a complaint. Soon afterward, her bosses assigned the 60-year-old supervisor to lift heavy tires at the plant. She believed this was to get back at her for the complaint. Soon she filed a lawsuit. It charged that Goodyear had unlawfully underpaid her $60,000 over the course of her career.

Ledbetter won the lawsuit. A jury awarded her $3.3 million, but a judge later reduced the amount to about $300,000.

However, Goodyear appealed the decision. The case ended up before the Supreme Court. In 2007, the Court decided—by a 5–4 majority—that Ledbetter wasn't entitled to receive any damages from Goodyear. The reason? The justices said that Title VII required people to bring a claim of pay discrimination within 180 days of the first instance of such discrimination.

Many people found the Supreme Court's decision hard to accept. Ledbetter hadn't known about her unfair treatment until many years after it began. How could she have filed a complaint in the time allowed?

Lawmakers decided to address the situation. In January 2009, Congress passed, and President Barack Obama signed, the Lilly Ledbetter Fair Pay Act. The law allows workers to file a complaint 180 days from the last instance of pay discrimination they believe they've suffered.

front of the fight against all forms of discrimination. In their view, racism or prejudice against gays is just as unacceptable as sexism. And, they say, all forms of oppression arise from similar impulses. Third-wave feminists tend to take a global outlook. They are concerned with stopping violence against women in the United States. They are equally concerned with stopping violence against women in Africa or Asia.

If second- and third-wave feminists don't always see eye to eye, they can agree on one thing: much remains to be done before full equality for women is achieved. Take the workplace, for instance. Many barriers to women's career success have been removed. Still, men continue to hold the great majority of the highest-level jobs. A 2010 survey by the Equal Employment Opportunity Commission (EEOC) found that women were the chief executive officers (CEOs) at just 13 of the 500 largest U.S. corporations (2.6 percent). Although women made up nearly half of the Fortune 500 workforce, they held only 26 percent of senior management positions and only 15.2 percent of corporate board seats. So women in the business world seem to face a "glass ceiling"—a level beyond which it is very difficult for them to rise.

The low numbers of female managers, board members, and CEOs are one issue. Pay across all job levels is another. U.S. Census Bureau data for 2011 indicate that women earn about 78 cents for every dollar earned by men. This is one reason more women than men are trapped in what has been called the "sticky floor" of poverty. Overall, the poverty rate for American women is nearly one-third higher than the poverty rate for American men. And women are poorer than men across all racial and ethnic groups.

Despite this, there is no denying that women have made huge strides toward equality. Not too long ago, women were widely believed to be unsuited for command and leadership positions. Today, that belief is discredited. Women have served—and served very capably—in many positions of authority.

The chapters that follow tell the stories of some groundbreaking women. Their pioneering achievements have opened the doors for other women to follow.

In September 1992, Dr. Mae C. Jemison (b. 1956) became the first African-American woman in space. A medical doctor who once served with the Peace Corps in Sierra Leone, Africa, Jemison spent more than 190 hours in space.

3

THE RIGHT STUFF

In 1959, the National Aeronautics and Space Administration (NASA) chose the first seven astronauts for America's space program. All had been military test pilots. And all were men. At the time, it seemed unthinkable that women might have the "right stuff" to be astronauts. But in 1963, a woman from the Soviet Union, Valentina Tereshkova, successfully completed a space mission. Couldn't American women do the same? NASA dismissed the idea. "Talk of an American spacewoman," a NASA spokesman said, "makes me sick to my stomach."

The idea of women at the highest levels of the military seemed equally absurd. By law, female officers couldn't be promoted to the rank of general or admiral. This was justified by the age-old view that women are overly emotional. Under the intense pressure of command, it was feared, women wouldn't be able to make logical decisions.

Today, the U.S. armed forces don't worry that women are emotionally unsuited for command. Nor does anyone suggest that women are too frail for the rigors of spaceflight. Pioneering women proved just how silly those notions were.

SALLY RIDE: AIMING FOR THE STARS

Born in 1951, Sally Kristen Ride showed an early talent for science. She was also an excellent athlete. As a junior tennis player, she was nationally ranked.

(Above) Five members of the first class of female astronauts are photographed during training, 1978. They included (left to right) Sally Ride, Judith A. Resnik, Anna L. Fisher, Kathryn D. Sullivan, and Rhea Seddon. All flew in space for NASA; Resnik died there when the space shuttle *Challenger* exploded shortly after liftoff in January 1986. (Bottom)

The sixth member of NASA's first female astronaut class, Shannon W. Lucid, spent more than 223 days in space. (Lucid's record for most time in space by a female astronaut was surpassed in 2007 by Peggy Whitson, who to date has spent over 377 days in space.)

Ride attended Stanford University in Palo Alto, California. She graduated with bachelor's degrees in English and physics. Ride went on to earn a master's degree in physics and a Ph.D. in astrophysics.

In 1978, Ride saw a newspaper ad that would change her life. NASA was seeking candidates for its astronaut program. Ride decided to give it a try. Out of 8,000 applicants, NASA chose 34 to fill its astronaut class. Ride was one of six women selected.

Ride went through intense training to become a mission specialist. On June 18, 1983, she blasted off aboard the space shuttle *Challenger*. This made her the first American woman in space. Ride and the other four members of the crew spent nearly a week in space. During that time, they tested the shuttle's robotic arm. They also performed various science experiments.

In 1984, Ride again traveled to space aboard the *Challenger*. The seven-person crew deployed an important satellite.

Ride was scheduled for a third space mission. But it was canceled after the *Challenger*

Official photo of Sally Ride, who in 1983 became the first American woman in space.

exploded shortly after takeoff on January 28, 1986. Ride served on the commission that investigated the causes of the accident.

Ride retired as an astronaut in 1987. But she served on the commission that examined the 2003 space shuttle *Columbia* disaster. Ride is the only person to have served on the *Challenger* and *Columbia* commissions.

Since her years at NASA, Dr. Ride has been a university professor. She also started a company whose goal is to make science fun for young students.

EILEEN COLLINS: TAKING COMMAND

The work of Sally Ride and other female astronauts paved the way for another barrier to be broken. By 1999, America's space shuttle program was approaching its 20th year. Almost four decades had passed since Alan Shepard became the first American in space. Yet no American woman had ever commanded a space mission. Eileen Collins would change that.

Eileen Marie Collins was born in 1956. She graduated from Syracuse University in 1978 with a bachelor's degree in mathematics and econom-

Official NASA photograph of Eileen M. Collins, who in 1998 became the first woman to command a Space Shuttle mission.

ics. Collins then entered the U.S. Air Force. She became a pilot.

By 1990, Collins had earned two master's degrees, had more than a decade of experience flying various types of military aircraft, and was enrolled in the elite Air Force Test Pilot School. NASA tapped her for its astronaut program.

Collins's flew shuttle missions in February 1995 and May 1997. On both occasions, she served as pilot.

When the shuttle *Columbia* blasted off on July 22, 1999, Collins was commander. The first space mission commanded by a woman deployed the Chandra X-ray Observatory. This special telescope allows scientists to see the invisible radiation given off by super-hot objects in the universe.

In 2005, Collins commanded another shuttle mission. It delivered supplies to the International Space Station. By the time of her retirement in 2006, Collins had logged more than a month's time in space on her four missions.

FAST FACT

In October 1984, Kathryn Sullivan became the first American woman to perform a space walk. Sullivan's space walk, officially called an extravehicular activity (EVA), lasted four hours.

JEANNE HOLM: OPENING UP THE WILD BLUE YONDER

Jeanne Holm was a true pioneer. She became the first female general in the U.S. Air Force. She later became the first woman in any branch of the armed services to reach the rank of major general. These groundbreaking achievements helped inspire other women who wanted to pursue a career in the military. But Holm didn't simply lead by example. She spent years actively tearing down obstacles to women's service in the air force.

Jeanne Marjorie Holm was born in 1921. In 1942, in the midst of World War II, she enlisted in what became the Women's Army Corps (WAC). The WAC provided assistance to the army, though its members didn't serve in combat. Holm commanded a WAC training regiment and, later, a hospital unit.

After the war's end in 1945, Holm settled back into civilian life. She attended college. But in 1948, Holm was recalled to active duty in the army. In 1949, she transferred to the air force. During the early stages of the Korean War (1950–53), she served as an assistant operations officer for a bomber unit.

Holm's abilities led her to be selected for the Air Command and Staff School at Maxwell Air Force Base in Montgomery, Alabama. She was the first woman ever to attend the school.

In 1965, Holm was promoted to full colonel. At the time, this was the highest military rank a woman could hold. Holm was appointed director of the Women in the Air Force (WAF). Established in 1948,

A photograph of Jeanne M. Holm taken in 1973, shortly after her promotion to Major General of the U.S. Air Force. She was the first female officer to achieve that rank in the U.S. military.

this corps severely restricted women's participation in the air force. The WAF could have just 300 officers and 4,000 enlisted women. Plus, a whole range of air force specialties (including pilot) were off limits to its members. After taking over as WAF director, however, Holm began pushing hard to eliminate these restrictions.

In 1967, the rules that prevented women in the armed forces from rising to the rank of general or admiral were lifted. Four years later, in July 1971, Holm was promoted to brigadier general. In 1973, she became the armed forces' first female major general.

General Holm greatly expanded opportunities for women in the air force. She more than doubled the size of the WAF. She succeeded in getting all but a handful of specialties opened up to women. "It was about equity," Holm would recall, "and it was about overturning traditional roles and what women could do in society."

Holm retired from the air force in 1975. The following year—thanks

Today, more than 50 women serve as generals or admirals in the U.S. armed forces. (Left) In 2008, Ann E. Dunwoody became the first woman in U.S. military history to become a four-star general. (Center) Lieutenant General Janet C. Wolfenbarger is vice commander of the Wright-Patterson Air Force Base. (Right) In 2006, Angela Salinas became the sixth woman, and first Hispanic female, to become a United States Marine Corps general officer.

FAST FACT

The Women's Armed Services Integration Act, which became law in 1948, made it possible for women to serve as permanent members of the regular U.S. armed forces. But the law barred them from advancing to the rank of general or admiral. It also capped female membership in any of the branches of the armed forces at 2 percent.

largely to her efforts—the WAF was abolished, and women were accepted into the air force as equals with men. Jeanne Holm died in February 2010.

DARLENE ISKRA: COMMAND ON THE HIGH SEAS

Darlene Iskra didn't set out to be a trailblazer. She simply wanted a good, steady job. But in the end, Iskra's ability and perseverance helped her achieve a huge milestone. She became the first female ship commander in the 200-year history of the U.S. Navy.

The year was 1979. Darlene Marie Iskra was 27 years old. She'd just been through a divorce and wanted to move on with her life. She also needed a job with benefits. Iskra enlisted in the navy. She was accepted into Officer Candidate School in Rhode Island. Iskra completed the four-month program. Next, she went to the Navy Diving and Salvage Training Center in Florida. In her class of 15, Iskra was one of two women.

The training to become a navy diver is physically grueling. "There were times I wanted to quit," Iskra would later admit. But she stuck with it, becoming one of the first female divers in the navy.

Iskra's naval education continued at the Surface Warfare Officer School in Rhode Island. There, she studied the essentials of operating a navy ship at sea. She learned about high-tech shipboard systems. She mastered navigation. She learned how to pilot a ship.

Lieutenant Commander Darlene M. Iskra (left) speaks with a sailor on the bridge of the USS *Opportune*, February 1991. Iskra was the first woman assigned to command a U.S. Navy ship.

In 1980, Iskra received her first ship assignment. She served as diving officer aboard the USS *Hector*, a navy repair ship. She held the rank of lieutenant. After a tour of duty with the *Hector*, Iskra reluctantly accepted an on-shore assignment. At the time, the navy didn't permit women to serve on combat ships. This made it very difficult for female officers to advance.

The navy eventually decided to relax its rules, however. By the mid-1980s, Iskra had been given another shipboard assignment. Her gift for supervision was noted by navy officials. And in December 1990, the navy tapped her to become its first female ship commander.

Iskra commanded the USS *Opportune*, a rescue and salvage ship. And she would have to take her ship into harm's way. In August 1990, the Middle Eastern country of Iraq had invaded its southern neighbor Kuwait. An international coalition, or alliance, led by the United States had formed to push Iraqi forces out of Kuwait. The fighting began in January 1991. It lasted six weeks. Throughout the conflict, today known as the Gulf War, the *Opportune* was deployed in the waters around the war zone. Commander Iskra and her crew stood ready to rescue any coalition sailors whose ships were attacked.

Iskra retired from the navy in 2000. She continues to advocate for increased opportunities for women in the armed forces.

4

EQUAL JUSTICE

The American system divides power among three branches of government. The legislative branch is made up of the two chambers of Congress, the Senate and House of Representatives. The legislative branch is responsible for creating the nation's laws.

The executive branch is headed by the president of the United States. It includes the president's cabinet as well as federal agencies and departments such as the Department of Defense, the Environmental Protection Agency, the Office of Management and Budget, and the Social Security Administration. The executive branch implements and enforces the laws created by Congress.

The judicial branch is the federal court system. The courts try legal cases. And, in the course of doing so, they must apply and interpret the law. Federal courts have the power to determine whether a law passed by Congress (or one of the 50 states) goes against the U.S. Constitution. If so, they can strike down the law. That is an extremely important power.

The judicial branch includes three levels. At the lowest level are district courts. Above them are the appellate (appeals) courts. At the top is the U.S. Supreme Court. Its nine justices get the final say on constitutional questions.

Supreme Court decisions have played a huge role in determining what the United States is like. But from 1789 until 1981, not a single woman had a voice on the Court. In the past three decades, however, four women have served.

SANDRA DAY O'CONNOR

Sandra Day O'Connor was born in El Paso, Texas, in 1930. She grew up there and on her parents' cattle ranch in eastern Arizona.

O'Connor attended Stanford University. In 1950, she graduated with a bachelor's degree in economics. She decided to get a law degree. At the time, this was still fairly uncommon for a woman. Of the 102 students in O'Connor's class at Stanford Law School, 97 were men. But O'Connor excelled. She won a position as an editor of the Stanford Law Review. She completed her studies in two years instead of the usual three. And she graduated third in her class.

Stanford is considered one of the country's best law schools. O'Connor's academic record was stellar. Yet only one law firm offered her a job. And the position wasn't as an attorney but rather as a legal secretary.

For about a year, O'Connor served as deputy attorney for the county of San Mateo, California. Then she spent three years in Germany, where her husband, John, served in the armed forces legal corps. The O'Connors returned to the United States in 1957. They settled in Phoenix, Arizona.

At the time, only about 3 percent of the nation's lawyers were female. O'Connor was still unable to get a job offer. So she started her own law

FAST FACT

The first majority decision Justice Sandra Day O'Connor wrote for the Supreme Court focused on sex discrimination. In *Mississippi University for Women v. Hogan*, the Court upheld the right of a man to attend a nursing school that had previously maintained a policy of admitting only women.

Sandra Day O'Connor is sworn in as a Supreme Court Justice by Chief Justice Warren Burger, September 25, 1981. In the center is her husband, John O'Connor.

firm with a partner. In 1960, however, she interrupted her law practice to become a full-time mother to her three young sons.

O'Connor returned to the workforce in 1965. She was appointed an assistant attorney general for the state of Arizona. She held that position until 1969. That year, a state senator resigned, and Arizona's governor appointed O'Connor to serve the remainder of his term. She later decided to run for the state senate seat. She won election twice.

O'Connor left the state senate in 1974. The following year, she was elected to a judgeship on the Maricopa County Superior Court. In 1979, she was appointed to the Arizona Court of Appeals.

In 1981, a seat on the U.S. Supreme Court became vacant with the resignation of Justice Potter Stewart. O'Connor was surprised to get a call from Attorney General William French Smith. Smith asked whether she

FAST FACT

According to a 2011 report by the Center for Women in Government and Civil Society, only 23 percent of the federal judges in the United States are female. Women hold 27 percent of state-level judgeships.

might be interested in a position on the Supreme Court. O'Connor joked, "It must be a secretarial position, is it not?"

President Ronald Reagan officially nominated O'Connor to the Supreme Court on August 19, 1981. The U.S. Senate quickly confirmed her. The vote was 99–0.

In September 1981, O'Connor took her seat as the Supreme Court's first female justice. She served close to 25 years. Legal scholars consider O'Connor a thoughtful, moderate justice. Sometimes she sided with the Supreme Court's more conservative members. Other times, she sided with the Court's liberal wing. Thus, she was often described as the "swing vote"—the justice who would end up deciding the cases over which the Supreme Court was closely divided. She wasn't entirely comfortable with that description. "I don't share the notion expressed by some in the media

FAST FACT

The attorney general of the United States heads the Department of Justice and is considered the nation's chief law enforcement officer. Janet Reno became the first woman to hold that important position. She was appointed by President Bill Clinton. Reno served from March 1993 to January 2001. In the history of the country, only one U.S. attorney general served longer.

in trying to describe the justices," she noted. "I try to do the best I can with each case, and leave it there."

Justice O'Connor announced her retirement in 2005. She stepped down in January of the following year.

RUTH BADER GINSBURG

For half of her time on the Supreme Court, Justice O'Connor had a female colleague. Ruth Bader Ginsburg joined the Court in 1993.

Born in 1933, she grew up Brooklyn, New York. She attended Cornell University, graduating first in her class. She married. Her husband, Martin, had completed a year at Harvard Law School in Cambridge, Massachusetts, when he was drafted into the army. After his service was completed, he returned to Harvard Law. And Ruth Bader Ginsburg enrolled there as well.

Very few women attended Harvard Law at the time. There were just nine women in Ruth Bader Ginsburg's class of more than 500. And the female presence wasn't exactly welcomed. During one lecture, the dean of the law school sneeringly asked the women how it felt to take spots that could have gone to qualified men. But Ginsburg refused to be intimidated. She shone in the classroom and won a position on the Harvard Law Review.

Ruth Bader Ginsburg became the second woman, and first Jewish woman, to serve on the Supreme Court. Appointed by President Bill Clinton, she took the oath of office on August 10, 1993.

Justice Sonia Sotomayor listens to a question during her 2009 confirmation hearing before the U.S. Senate. On August 8, 2009, she took the oath of office, becoming the third female justice, as well as the first Latina, to serve on the Supreme Court.

After graduating from Harvard Law School, Ginsburg's husband got a job in New York City. She transferred to Columbia Law School so that she and her daughter could be with him in New York. Ginsburg graduated at the top of her class at Columbia.

In the years that followed, she taught at Rutgers University Law School and then at Columbia Law School. She also worked on legal issues involving women. Ginsburg would argue six women's-rights cases before the U.S. Supreme Court.

In 1972, Ginsburg helped launch the Women's Rights Project of the American Civil Liberties Union (ACLU). The next year, she became the ACLU's chief lawyer. She served in that role until 1980. Ginsburg left the ACLU to take a position as a judge on the U.S. Court of Appeals for the District of Columbia Circuit.

In 1993, President Bill Clinton nominated Ginsburg to the Supreme Court. She won easy confirmation by the U.S. Senate. She took her seat in August 1993.

During her time on the Supreme Court, Ginsburg has won a reputation as a staunch defender of women's rights. She has also been a champion of civil liberties.

A GREATER FEMALE VOICE ON THE COURT

Two Supreme Court justices retired during the first two years of Barack Obama's presidency. President Obama filled both seats with women, Sonia Sotomayor and Elena Kagan. With Ruth Bader Ginsburg continuing to serve, this meant that three of the Supreme Court's nine justices were women.

Chief Justice John G. Roberts, Jr., administers the Constitutional oath to Elena Kagan in the Justices' Conference Room on Saturday, August 7, 2010. Jeffrey P. Minear, counselor to the Chief Justice, holds the Bible.

Sonia Sotomayor, who joined the Court in 2009, was born in New York City in 1954. She is the first Latina justice: both her parents were Puerto Rican. Sotomayor is a graduate of Princeton University and Yale Law School. She had wide legal experience before joining the nation's highest court. She served as an assistant district attorney. She was a federal judge at the district court and appellate court level.

Elena Kagan is also from New York City. She was born in 1960. She graduated from Princeton University and Harvard Law School. Kagan was a professor at the University of Chicago Law School. From 1995 to 1999, she served in the administration of President Bill Clinton. She became the first female dean of the Harvard Law School in 2003. Six years later, she notched another first: she was the first woman to serve as U.S. solicitor general. The solicitor general is responsible for representing the federal government in cases before the Supreme Court. In 2010, Kagan went from presenting arguments before the Court to hearing arguments as a member of the Court.

5

LEADERS IN GOVERNMENT AND POLITICS

I n 1966, NOW called for women to be brought into "full participation in the mainstream of American society." A look at today's political scene shows just how much progress has been made toward achieving this goal. Yes, men still greatly outnumber women in high government offices. Yes, the United States has yet to elect a female president. But this much is certain: Women are now front and center on the national political stage.

As state governors and as members of Congress, women have confidently added their voices to America's ongoing debates. They have put forth their ideas for making the country better. They have brought their talents to bear on solving problems. They have led.

These female leaders represent the full spectrum of political views. They are liberals and conservatives. They are Democrats, Republicans, and Independents. Some are widely admired. Others come in for harsh criticism from their political opponents. But that, too, can be seen as a sign of progress. More and more, women in politics are treated no differently from men. Ideas and actions matter. Gender isn't important.

In the 112th Congress, which began in 2011, women chaired eight committees. These included committees involved in what in the past would certainly have been considered "men's business." For example, the Senate Intelligence Committee was chaired by Dianne Feinstein, a Democrat from California. Patty Murray, a Democrat from Washington, headed the Senate Veterans' Affairs Committee. Representative Ileana Ros-Lehtinen, a Republican from Florida, chaired the House Foreign Affairs Committee. Each of these women has a fascinating life story. Each has spent decades in public service. And each could offer important lessons about women and politics. But the rise of women in American politics is perhaps best illustrated by the careers of Nancy Pelosi and Hillary Rodham Clinton.

Clinton ran for president in 2008. While she wasn't the first woman to do so, she was the first who had a realistic chance of winning. In fact, she ran neck-and-neck with Barack Obama in the race for the Democratic Party's nomination. And that changed the way a lot of Americans thought about the idea of a woman in the White House. It no longer seemed so improbable.

During the 111th Congress, Pelosi served as Speaker of the House of Representatives. That's the top leadership position in the House. It's one of the most powerful positions in the entire government.

THE PATH TO CONGRESS

The future Speaker of the House was born Nancy Patricia D'Alesandro on March 26, 1940. She was the youngest of six children. She grew up in Baltimore, Maryland.

FAST FACT

The Constitution specifies that the Speaker of the House becomes president of the United States in the event both the president and vice president die while in office.

Politics were a frequent topic of conversation in the D'Alesandro household. Thomas D'Alesandro Jr., Nancy's father, was a well-known figure in the Democratic Party. He held office at the local, state, and national levels. At the time of Nancy's birth, he was in the first of five straight terms representing Maryland's 3rd Congressional District in the U.S. House of Representatives. Later, he served as Baltimore's mayor for 12 years. Nancy's brother, Thomas D'Alesandro III, would also be elected mayor of Baltimore.

Nancy attended Trinity College in Washington, D.C. She graduated in 1962 with a degree in political science. A year later, she married Paul Pelosi, a businessman. They lived in New York for several years. Then they moved to San Francisco, Paul Pelosi's hometown.

Representative Nancy Pelosi of California served as the 60th Speaker of the United States House of Representatives from 2007 to 2011. She was the first woman to hold this important Congressional office.

Nancy Pelosi didn't enter politics right away. She stayed at home to raise the five children she and her husband had. When the last of those children started school, she began volunteering for Democratic Party causes.

Beginning in the mid-1970s, Pelosi was elected to a series of positions with the California Democratic Party. In 1981, she won the post of state party chair. She met the state's most powerful Democratic leaders.

Pelosi was especially close to Sala Burton, who served in the U.S. House of Representatives. In 1983, Burton was appointed to serve out the term of her husband, Philip, who died in office. She twice won election on her own.

FAST FACT

In 1984, Geraldine Ferraro became the first woman on a major party's presidential ticket. Democratic presidential nominee Walter Mondale chose the congresswoman from New York as his vice presidential running mate. But the Democrats were soundly defeated by the Republicans, President Ronald Reagan and Vice President George H. W. Bush.

In 1986, Sala Burton was diagnosed with an incurable cancer. She asked Nancy Pelosi to run for her seat in Congress. Pelosi agreed. Burton died in February 1987. In June, Pelosi won a special election to fill her seat.

RISING STAR

San Francisco is a Democratic stronghold. The 8th Congressional District, which Pelosi represents, hasn't sent a Republican to Washington since 1948. Every two years, Pelosi easily won reelection. With each term she served, she gained more influence among Democrats in the House of Representatives. She was assigned to two important committees, Intelligence and Appropriations. (The Appropriations Committee decides how much money the U.S. government will spend in the various areas of the budget.) Among the issues Pelosi focused on were health care and education.

Pelosi steadily won the respect of her fellow House Democrats. In 2001, they elected her to an important leadership position: Democratic whip. In the party that holds fewer seats in the House of Representatives—as the Democrats did in 2001—whip is the second-highest position. Only the minority leader is higher. The whip tries to maintain unity within the party, making sure that members vote with their party on important bills. The job requires great people skills. Pelosi had those skills.

In November 2002, House Democrats showed their confidence in

Today, some of the most powerful members of the U.S. Senate are women. (Left) Barbara Boxer of California has served in the U.S. Senate since 1993. As the Democratic Party's Chief Deputy Whip, she is a key member of the party's Senate leadership structure. (Center) In 1992, Patty Murray became the first woman elected to the U.S. Senate from the state of Washington. In 2011, Murray began a second two-year term as chairman of the Democratic Senatorial Campaign Committee, an important position in which she helps to get the party's candidates elected to the Senate. (Right) Susan Collins, a senator from Maine, has a reputation as a moderate Republican.

Nancy Pelosi. They elected her their leader. It was the first time ever that a woman had served as a party leader in Congress. Pelosi remained House minority leader for four years.

SPEAKER OF THE HOUSE

The 2006 congressional elections brought a major shift in power. Voters were unhappy with the policies of President George W. Bush, a Republican. They were unhappy with the Republican Party in general. Democrats won big at the polls.

The elections gave Democrats control of Congress. When the 110th Congress convened in January 2007, Nancy Pelosi was elected Speaker of the House of Representatives. That is the number-one leadership position in the House. The Speaker controls which bills get brought to the floor of the House for voting. Never before had a woman held this very important position. Pelosi referred to that fact in a speech she made upon becoming Speaker:

> This is a historic moment—for the Congress, and for the women of this country. It is a moment for which we have waited more than 200 years. Never losing faith, we waited through the many years of struggle to achieve our rights. But women weren't just waiting; women were working. Never losing faith, we worked to redeem the promise of America, that all men and women are created equal.

Pelosi aroused strong feelings—positive and otherwise—during her time as Speaker. Democrats for the most part considered her a strong, capable leader who stood up for liberal values. By contrast, many

During the 2008 presidential campaign, Nancy Pelosi worked to defeat another high-profile female politician—Alaska governor Sarah Palin, who was the vice presidential candidate of the Republican Party.

Republicans painted her in the harshest of terms. Some slammed her for opposing President Bush's war policy in Iraq. Others accused her of having radical views. Still others said she was shrill and pushy—descriptions that are often applied to powerful women but not to powerful men.

Pelosi won reelection as Speaker in 2008. That year also brought a Democrat, Barack Obama, to the presidency. With Democrats in control of both chambers of Congress as well as the White House, many people expected the passage of a flood of new Democratic-sponsored legislation. Under Pelosi's leadership, the House did, in fact, pass a vast array of bills. But more than 300 of these bills died in the Senate. There, Republicans blocked bills from being voted on through a procedure known as the filibuster.

Republicans regained control of the House of Representatives in the 2010 elections. This ended Pelosi's time as Speaker. In January 2011, she handed the leadership gavel to Republican John Boehner of Ohio.

Pelosi's time as Speaker wasn't long by historical standards. But a catalog of the major legislation passed under her leadership is impressive. That legislation included a major overhaul of the nation's health care system, financial reform, a large expansion of health insurance for children, the Lilly Ledbetter Fair Pay Act, and more. "We're looking at an extraordinary set of accomplishments over a brief period of time," noted congressional historian Norman Ornstein. "[Nancy Pelosi] ranks with the most consequential speakers, certainly in the last 75 years."

HILLARY CLINTON: EARLY YEARS

Hillary Clinton has certainly put her stamp on American politics and government. She has been America's First Lady. She has served as a U.S. senator. She has run for president. And she has been secretary of state, the country's chief diplomat.

She was born Hillary Diane Rodham in Chicago on October 26, 1947. She attended Wellesley College in Massachusetts, graduating in 1969 with a degree in political science. She then entered Yale Law School.

While at Yale, she volunteered to provide legal help to poor people. She also did research on children in the legal system and volunteered to represent victims of child abuse. Helping vulnerable children would become a lifelong concern.

During her second year at Yale, she met Bill Clinton, a law student from Arkansas. The two fell in love. They would eventually move to Little Rock, Arkansas, and marry in 1975. There, Bill Clinton began a political career. Hillary Clinton set up a nonprofit organization to help children and families. Later, she became a partner at a Little Rock law firm.

In 1978, Bill Clinton was elected governor of Arkansas. In 1980, he failed in a reelection bid. That same year, Hillary Clinton gave birth to the couple's only child, a daughter they named Chelsea.

In 1982, Bill Clinton ran for governor again and won. He would serve continuously until 1992. While he was governor, Bill Clinton asked his wife to work on important state issues. They included public-education reform and health care reform.

IN THE WHITE HOUSE AND THE SENATE

In 1992, Bill Clinton ran for president of the United States. He won.

As he'd done while governor of Arkansas, Clinton soon assigned his wife an important mission for his administration. Hillary Clinton chaired a task force on reforming the U.S. health care system. The goal was to ensure that all Americans received health insurance coverage. But conservative critics quickly cried foul. They said it wasn't right that the First Lady be given a role in policy making. They pointed out that the American people had elected Bill Clinton, not Hillary Clinton. The White House had a logical response: the president appointed many people to advise him. Hillary Clinton was like any other unelected adviser.

But the health care task force was the target of bitter criticism. Some of it was clearly political. Some stemmed from the task force's secrecy. The health care plan was put together behind closed doors, with no input from members of Congress. And in the end, Congress balked at passing the plan.

Despite this defeat—and despite a series of controversies that rocked Bill Clinton's presidency—Hillary Clinton maintained a high public profile. In fact, historians consider her one of the most active First Ladies in U.S.

"When I was asked what it means to be a woman running for president, I always gave the same answer: that I was proud to be running as a woman but I was running because I thought I'd be the best President," Hillary Clinton said in a speech conceding defeat in the Democratic Party primary, June 2008. "But I am a woman, and like millions of women, I know there are still barriers and biases out there, often unconscious. . . . Although we weren't able to shatter that highest, hardest glass ceiling this time, thanks to you, it's got about 18 million cracks in it. And the light is shining through like never before, filling us all with the hope and the sure knowledge that the path will be a little easier next time. That has always been the history of progress in America."

history. She traveled the world promoting women's rights and human rights in general. She spearheaded efforts to strengthen protections for adopted and foster children in the United States. She was a tireless champion for American families. "For better or worse, I was outspoken," Clinton recalled in her book *Living History*. "I represented a fundamental change in the way women functioned in our society."

Bill Clinton served two terms as president. As her husband's time in the White House was winding down, Hillary Clinton decided that she wasn't quite ready to retire from public service. In 2000, she became the first First Lady ever to run for elective office. She defeated Republican Rick Lazio to win a seat in the U.S. Senate from the state of New York.

DIPLOMATS-IN-CHIEF

It took more than 200 years after the founding of the United States for the nation to have its first female secretary of state. But, starting in 1997, three of the four people to hold this important office were women.

Madeleine Albright was secretary of state during the second term of President Bill Clinton. She served from 1997 to 2001.

Madeleine Albright

When he became president in 2001, George W. Bush picked Colin Powell as his chief diplomat. During his second term, however, Bush tapped Condoleezza Rice. She'd been his national security adviser. Rice served from 2005 until 2009.

Barack Obama looked to a former rival to become his secretary of state. Hillary Clinton took over at the State Department in January 2010.

Condoleeza Rice

Supporters line up to cheer at a California event during Hillary Clinton's 2008 candidacy for the Democratic Party's presidential nomination.

Many people, even former critics, were impressed by Clinton's performance in the Senate. She won high marks for her hard work. She took great pains to educate herself in subjects with which she was less familiar, such as national defense and foreign policy. Fellow senators considered her thoughtful and careful.

In 2006, Clinton won reelection to the Senate in a landslide. Soon, however, she set her sights on another office: the presidency.

RACE FOR THE WHITE HOUSE

By early 2007, President George W. Bush was entering his final two years in office. He was very unpopular. So, too, was his Republican Party. Many political experts believed a Democrat would have an excellent chance to win the 2008 presidential election.

Minnesota congresswoman Michele Bachmann speaks to supporters during her 2012 presidential campaign.

On January 20, 2007, Hillary Clinton announced her candidacy for president. She was considered the favorite to win the Democratic Party's nomination. But the field soon became crowded with contenders.

The primaries—state-by-state contests in which voters cast ballots for a candidate from their party—began in early January 2008. Within six weeks, two candidates had separated themselves from the rest of the Democratic field. Both were running historic campaigns. Hillary Clinton sought to become America's first female president. Barack Obama, a first-term U.S. senator from Illinois, wanted to be the country's first African-American president.

The campaign was hard fought. The candidates presented a study in contrasts. Clinton could claim years of political experience on the national stage. The relatively untested Obama promised to bring change to Washington. Before the primaries were over, each candidate would tally more than 18 million votes. But in the end, Obama held the edge. He secured the Democratic Party's nomination. And, in November 2008, he won the presidency by defeating Republican John McCain.

Although it fell short, Hillary Clinton's campaign for president changed the American political landscape. Never before had a woman won a single presidential primary. Clinton won more than 20. Never before had a woman mounted a presidential campaign with a realistic chance of success. Perhaps most important, many Americans can now imagine a female chief executive.

As President Obama prepared his 2012 reelection bid, a couple of women emerged as possible Republican opponents. Sarah Palin, the former governor of Alaska, had been John McCain's vice presidential running mate in 2008. Palin's supporters encouraged her to run for president. In 2011, Michele Bachmann, a five-term member of the U.S. House of Representatives from Minnesota, launched her presidential campaign. After a good showing early, her support faded and she ended her campaign after the Iowa caucuses in January 2012.

As for Hillary Clinton, she became a key member of President Obama's cabinet. On January 21, 2009, she was sworn in as the 67th Secretary of State.

CHAPTER NOTES

p. 10:   "race, color, religion, sex, or national origin." *United States Code: The Public Health and Welfare*, Vol. 25, Title 42 (2006), p. 444.

p. 12:   "reasonably necessary to the normal operation," Ibid, p. 452.

p. 13:   "head and master," Laurence C. Nolan and Lynn D. Wardle, *Fundamental Principles of Family Law*, 2nd ed. (Buffalo, N.Y.: William S. Hein & Co., 2006), p. 395.

p. 17:   "absolute tyranny." The Declaration of Sentiments, available at Women's Rights National Historical Park, http://www.nps.gov/wori/historyculture/declaration-of-sentiments.htm

p. 20:   "We can no longer ignore . . ." Betty Friedan, *The Feminine Mystique* (New York: Dell, 1963), p. 78.

p. 20:   "The purpose of NOW . . ." The National Organization for Women's 1966 Statement of Purpose, reprinted in Lynne E. Ford, *Encyclopedia of Women and American Politics* (New York: Facts on File, 2008), p. 575.

p. 27:   "Talk of an American spacewoman . . ." Claire Booth Luce, "She Orbits Over the Sex Barrier . . . But Some People Simply Never Get the Message," *Life* 54, no. 26 (June 28, 1963), p. 31.

p. 32:   "It was about equality . . ." Jeanne M. Holm, quoted in Douglas Martin, "Jeanne Holm Dies at 88: A Pioneer in the Air Force" *New York Times* (March 2, 2010), p. B13.

p. 33:   "There were times . . ." Darlene Iskra, quoted in Erin Jennings, "Officer and a Gentlewoman: Darlene Iskra Made History as First Female Commander of a U.S. Navy ship," *North Kitsap Herald* (March 18, 2011). http://www.pnwlocalnews.com/kitsap/nkh/lifestyle/118250074.html

p. 38:   "It must be a secretarial..." Sandra Day O'Connor, quoted in Joan Biskupic, *Sandra Day O'Connor: How the First Woman on the Supreme Court Became Its Most Influential Justice* (New York: Ecco, 2005), p. 4.

p. 38:   "I don't share the notion . . ." Sandra Day O'Connor, transcript of interview on *Dateline*, NBC News, January 25, 2002.

p. 43: "full participation in . . ." The National Organization for Women's 1966 Statement of Purpose, reprinted in Ford, *Encyclopedia of Women and American Politics*, p. 575.

p. 49: "We're looking at an extraordinary set . . ." Norman Ornstein, quoted in Linda Burstyn, "Watch Out, John—Nancy's Still on the Job," *Ms. Magazine* (Winter 2011). http://msmagazine.com/blog/blog/2011/01/05/watch-out-john-nancys-still-on-the-job/

p. 51: "When I was asked . . ." Hillary Clinton, "Hillary Clinton Endorses Barack Obama," *New York Times* (June 7, 2008). http://www.nytimes.com/2008/06/07/us/politics/07text-clinton.html?pagewanted=all

p. 52 "For better or worse, I . . ." Hillary Rodham Clinton, *Living History* (New York: Simon & Schuster, 2003), p. 110.

In 1983, Grace M. Hopper (1906–1992) became the first woman to achieve the rank of Commodore (Rear Admiral) in the U.S. Navy.

CHRONOLOGY

1920: In August, the 19th Amendment is ratified. It guarantees women in the United States equal voting rights with men.

1963: *The Feminine Mystique*, by Betty Friedan, is published.

1964: The Civil Rights Act of 1964 becomes law. It prohibits discrimination in the workplace based on "race, color, religion, sex, or national origin."

1966: The National Organization for Women (NOW) is founded.

1981: Sandra Day O'Connor becomes the first woman Supreme Court justice.

1982: The Equal Rights Amendment fails to win ratification.

1984: Geraldine Ferraro becomes the first woman on the presidential ticket of a major American political party. She is the Democratic nominee for vice president.

1993: Ruth Bader Ginsburg becomes the second woman appointed to the U.S. Supreme Court.

1997: In January, Madeleine Albright becomes the first woman to serve as U.S. secretary of state.

2001: Nancy Pelosi, a Democrat from California, is elected House Democratic whip. It is the highest rank a woman has reached in the history of the U.S. Congress.

2005: Condoleezza Rice becomes the first African-American woman to serve as U.S. secretary of state.

2007: Pelosi becomes Speaker of the U.S. House of Representatives. She is the first woman to hold the top leadership position in the House.

2008: Senator Hillary Clinton finishes second to Barack Obama in the race for the Democratic Party's presidential nomination. John McCain, the Republican nominee for president, selects Alaska governor Sarah Palin as his running mate.

2009: Hillary Clinton becomes the 67th Secretary of State.

2011: As of January, women held 17 of 100 U.S. Senate seats, 71 of 435 seats in the U.S. House of Representatives, and 6 of the 50 state governorships.

GLOSSARY

amendment—a change to a law or governing document, such as the U.S. Constitution.

attorney general—the chief law officer for the federal government or one of the states.

civil disobedience—refusal to obey laws or rules, as a means of protest.

discrimination—unequal treatment of individuals based on their gender, race, ethnicity, or other group identity.

gender—the state of being male or female; sex.

glass ceiling—barriers to the attainment of top-level positions, especially those faced by women.

sexism—the belief that women are inferior to men; discrimination against women.

suffrage—the right to vote.

suffragists—people who advocated that the right to vote be guaranteed to women.

Supreme Court—the highest court in the United States, with final authority to decide whether laws violate the U.S. Constitution.

FURTHER READING

FOR YOUNGER READERS

Bausum, Ann. *With Courage and Cloth: Winning the Fight for a Woman's Right to Vote*. Washington, D.C.: National Geographic Children's Books, 2004.

Kimmel, Elizabeth Cody. *Ladies First: 40 Daring American Women Who Were Second to None*. Washington, D.C.: National Geographic, 2005.

Krull, Kathleen, and Kathryn Hewitt, illustrator. *Lives of Extraordinary Women: Rulers, Rebels (And What the Neighbors Thought)*. San Diego: Harcourt, 2000.

Stone, Tanya Lee. *Almost Astronauts: 13 Women Who Dared to Dream*. Somerville, Mass.: Candlewick Press, 2009.

Wade, Linda R. *Sally Ride: The Story of the First American Female in Space*. Bear, Del.: Mitchell Lane Publishers, 2002.

FOR OLDER READERS

Albright, Madeleine. *Madam Secretary: A Memoir*. New York: Hyperion, 2003.

Biskupic, Joan. *Sandra Day O'Connor: How the First Woman on the Supreme Court Became Its Most Influential Justice*. New York: Ecco, 2005.

Clinton, Hillary Rodham. *Living History*. New York: Simon & Schuster, 2003.

Collins, Gail. *When Everything Changed: The Amazing Journey of American Women from 1960 to Present*. New York: Little, Brown, and Co., 2009.

Friedan, Betty. *Life So Far: A Memoir*. New York: Simon & Schuster, 2000.

Kornblut, Anne E. *Notes from the Cracked Ceiling: Hillary Clinton, Sarah Palin, and What It Will Take for a Woman to Win*. New York: Crown Publishers, 2009.

McMillen, Sally G. *Seneca Falls and the Origins of the Women's Rights Movement*. New York: Oxford University Press, 2008.

Norton, Mary Beth, and Ruth M. Alexander, eds. *Major Problems in American Women's History*, 4th ed. Boston: Houghton Mifflin, 2007.

Peters, Ronald M., and Cindy S. Rosenthal. *Speaker Nancy Pelosi and the New American Politics*. New York: Oxford University Press, 2010.

INTERNET RESOURCES

http://womenincongress.house.gov

This site provides information about female members of Congress, past and present.

http://www.womensmemorial.org/Education/timeline.html

A timeline of American women in military service, from the Revolutionary War to the present.

http://www.now.org

The home page of the National Organization for Women (NOW).

http://www.msmagazine.com/mar03/steinem1.asp

An essay by activist and *Ms. Magazine* founder Gloria Steinem titled "Feminist To Do List."

INDEX

Numbers in **bold italics** refer to captions.

CONTRIBUTORS

ELIZABETH KING HUMPHREY is a writer and editor living in Wilmington, N.C., surrounded by her husband and three children. Once a television news producer and computer software trainer, she has worked for Associated Press and CBS News. For many years, Elizabeth lived and worked in Prague, Johannesburg, and London. Originally from Colorado, she received her bachelor's degree in political science from Columbia University and her master's in creative writing from the University of North Carolina Wilmington.

Senior Consulting Editor **A. PAGE HARRINGTON** is executive director of the Sewall-Belmont House and Museum, on Capitol Hill in Washington, D.C. The Sewall-Belmont House celebrates women's progress toward equality—and explores the evolving role of women and their contributions to society—through educational programs, tours, exhibits, research, and publications.

The historic National Woman's Party (NWP), a leader in the campaign for equal rights and women's suffrage, owns, maintains, and interprets the Sewall-Belmont House and Museum. One of the premier women's history sites in the country, this National Historic Landmark houses an extensive collection of suffrage banners, archives, and artifacts documenting the continuing effort by women and men of all races, religions, and backgrounds to win voting rights and equality for women under the law.

The Sewall-Belmont House and Museum and the National Woman's Party are committed to preserving the legacy of Alice Paul, founder of the NWP and author of the Equal Rights Amendment, and telling the untold stories for the benefit of scholars, current and future generations of Americans, and all the world's citizens.